THE KINGDOM
of
HAPPINESS

By
JEDDU KRISHNAMURTI

BONI & LIVERIGHT · NEW YORK

1 9 2 7

Kessinger Publishing's Rare Reprints
Thousands of Scarce and Hard-to-Find Books!

．　　　　　　．　　　　　　．
．　　　　　　．　　　　　　．
．　　　　　　．　　　　　　．
．　　　　　　．　　　　　　．
．　　　　　　．　　　　　　．
．　　　　　　．　　　　　　．
．　　　　　　．　　　　　　．
．　　　　　　．　　　　　　．
．　　　　　　．　　　　　　．
．　　　　　　．　　　　　　．
．　　　　　　．　　　　　　．
．　　　　　　．　　　　　　．
．　　　　　　．　　　　　　．
．　　　　　　．　　　　　　．
．　　　　　　．　　　　　　．
．　　　　　　．　　　　　　．
．　　　　　　．　　　　　　．
．　　　　　　．　　　　　　．
．　　　　　　．　　　　　　．

We kindly invite you to view our extensive catalog list at:
http://www.kessinger.net

FOREWORD

I HAVE been asked to write a foreword to the following pages. Frankly they do not need it, but perhaps some sort of an explanation is necessary for their appearance.

They are talks given to certain friends of mine at the Castle of Eerde, Ommen, Holland. The Castle is of the early eighteenth century style of building, and it is supposed to be one of the best specimens of that period. It certainly is one of the most beautiful places that I know. Everything in the Castle is of that period, and is in perfect condition. The Gobelins are wonderful, and they give an atmosphere of ancient dignity and beauty. Great trees two or three hundred years old surround the Castle, and their mighty tops disappear into the clouds, and there you can hear strange whisperings.

The place is full of charm and happiness, and my talks naturally turned on that eternal subject.

J. KRISHNAMURTI.

[v]

NOTE

I may add to the above that the conditions described were the most favorable possible for the presence of the World Teacher's influence. Krishnaji was surrounded by a small group of eager students, believing in his inspiration and joyously welcoming the presence of the Lord. Readers will recognize the depth of wisdom, the striking originality, the exquisite diction of this really wonderful book. The wise will prize it, the other-wise will do as they please.

ANNIE BESANT.

CONTENTS

THE KINGDOM OF HAPPINESS

I

THE VOICE OF INTUITION

I WANT, if I can, to put before you certain ideas which you should cultivate and which would give you a definite and intelligent conception of true spiritual life. I think all of you realize that to create, as you must create if you would live, there must be struggle and discontent; and in guiding these to their fruition, you must cultivate your own point of view, your own tendencies, your own abilities; and for this I desire to arouse in each that Voice, that Tyrant, the only true guide that will help you to create. Most of you prefer —it is a much easier way—to copy. Most of you like to follow. Most of you find it much easier not to cultivate your own tendencies, your own qualities, your own natures, but rather to follow blindly. And I think you will agree with me that it is fatal for the development of the Voice. The noblest guide each of us has is this Voice, this Tyrant, this Intuition; and it is in cultivating, in ennobling,

[13]

and in perfecting this, that we arrive at the goal—our own goal.

In cultivating this Voice till it becomes the one Tyrant, the one Voice which we obey, we must find out our goal and work unceasingly for its attainment. Now what is this goal? To me it is this: I want to attain the Ultimate Truth. I want to reach a state where I know for myself that I have conquered, that I have attained, that I am the embodiment of that Truth, so that all the little struggles, the little turmoils, the little disturbances of life— though they have their value—do not upset me, do not cloud the vision of the Truth. And in attaining this Truth I attain at the same time what I desire—the peace, the perfect tranquillity of mind and of emotions. This is the goal for me. The first essential is the strengthening of this Voice, in each of us, which asserts itself from time to time. And in cultivating and in ennobling the Intuition we must learn to think and act for ourselves. The cultivation of this voice of intuition means a life according to its edicts.

Imitation has nothing to do with the beautiful; art consists, not in the copy of Nature, as it is, but in the nobleness of the symbol of that Nature which it represents. So each one of us has to be an artist, an artist who creates for himself, because he has been thrilled by a glimpse of the Vision. You will find that true and great artists, true and great teachers, have not the sense of exclusiveness; they embody all things, are part of all things. We must be varied in order to produce the perfect thing. A garden full of roses, however beautiful, becomes monotonous. You may have the most perfect roses of many types and colors, but if they are all roses, the garden lacks a sense of beauty. There is a tendency in each one of us to become like the others. We all desire to conform to a certain type and make ourselves fit into molds not of our own making. This is fatal to the development of perfect intuition. And yet we must never forget that we shall all meet in the Kingdom of Happiness.

We have a tendency all through our nationalism, our forms of worship, to think that we are different from other people; we treat the world as outside of us and we become exclusive in our outlook. We shall be destroying instead of creating if we have such a limited vision, such narrow ideas. I want, if I can, to rouse in each one of you this Voice, that shall guide you along the line you want to follow, that is your own life, the path of your own making. And as long as you obey that Voice, that Intuition, you cannot err; it is in trying to follow the orders, the ideas, the visions of others that you go wrong. I can point out my ideal of Truth, of perfect peace, of loving-kindness, but you must struggle and arrive at it for yourselves. I can lay down the principles of Truth, but through your own Voice, through the obeying of that Voice, you must develop your own intuition, your own ideas, and so you will come to the goal where we shall all meet.

This is for me the big thing in life. I do not want to obey anybody, it does not matter who he is, so long as I do not feel he is right. I do not want to hide behind the screen which veils the Truth. I do not want to have beliefs to which I cannot respond and to which I cannot give my soul and my heart and my whole being. Instead of being the ordinary and the mediocre, you will listen to this Voice, cultivate this Intuition, and so discover new avenues of life instead of being swept aimlessly along the path of another.

In realizing this ideal, as I said, you must develop your Intuition. A perfect harmony of emotions and of mind is essential, so that intuition, the voice of your true self, can express itself. Intuition is the whisper of the soul; Intuition is the guiding word in our life. The more we harmonize our strong feelings and keen mind by perfecting and purifying them, the more likely are we to hear that Voice, the Intuition which is common to all, the Intuition which is of humanity and not of one particular individual. You must have strong feelings, whether of love, of intense happiness, of real kindness. A person who has no feelings at all is useless; whereas if he has strong feelings, even if they be of the wrong kind, he can always train them to become refined and perfect. It is the person who is hard and indifferent that cannot create, destroy, or construct. You will find that a great destroyer is never a small person—there is something wonderful about him; a great lover is never mediocre or small. The more feelings you have, the better; but at the same time you must learn control, because emotions are like weeds, and unless you restrain them, they will spoil the garden. If you have weak emotions, but

[17]

give them nourishment day by day, they will strengthen and grow. The idea that we should have no feelings and emotions is absurd and unspiritual. The more you are bubbling over with feelings, the better; but you will find you have to control them, and if you do not, you suffer. If you do not control them you are going farther away from your Intuition, you are wandering away on the bypaths instead of walking on the main road towards your goal. Have tremendous feelings. Sport yourselves with them.

Do not be negative, but go out and be adventurous. I feel this so strongly, because we all tend to become of one type; we all want to think along the same lines, we all want to flock around the same person, we all fear that if we do not belong to this movement or to that we shall not advance. What is advancement? It is your own happiness—advancement is only a word. I would rather be happy than gain all the petty satisfaction that the world can give. What does it matter to which religion you belong, what glories you bear, so long as you feel really happy and can keep your goal absolutely clear and undimmed? Imagine for the moment the Lord Buddha and

[18]

His disciples. They were the great exceptions of their Age. They all had one Master,
one goal, one ideal, and that was He. And
yet they had, every one of them, the spark
of genius; they were not mediocre, because
they followed Him who was the exception,
the flower of humanity, and such examples
must we all become.

II

INTEREST AND ENTHUSIASM

I WOULD like to impress upon you the importance of taking interest in life, because without interest you cannot do anything. You *must* be intensely interested. I am interested in all things because all life around me gives me understanding. There is nothing else for me in life but to find Truth, to find Happiness, to find peace and tranquillity.

To be really interested you must have your mind and emotions alive all day long, active and not dormant. I would I could give you some of the interest I feel, so that you could awaken that interest in yourselves. For if you have not that interest, that desire to find, that longing to attain, that inclination to set aside everything to reach the ultimate, you will not be able to learn to sacrifice. That interest only comes if you are truly civilized. To the savage who is entering the first stage of life, to whom everything is new, who is accumulating karma, who is learning to suffer,

[20]

who is beginning to create, to that savage there is only one narrow interest in life. He wants to acquire, to experience, to taste everything physical; whereas the civilized and cultured person, through the evolution of many lives and through his past karma, has stored up knowledge, experience, intuition, and power of discrimination. He is all the time discarding the things that are not important; and to him this is the one way to awaken interest in the desire to find Truth.

Now to you and to me, that interest must be in its essence as thrilling and vital as it is to the barbarian who is just beginning to taste the pleasures and sensations of life. But you have set yourselves on a different path possessing new desires, because you have already passed through the stage of the savage to whom the physical every-day happenings of life are all-engrossing. He is still creating karma for himself, whereas you should be freeing yourselves from it. You should be strengthening your will and guiding your desires so that you can learn to follow the Tyrant Voice. The only way to hear and to follow that Voice, your guide for all time, is through enthusiasm. If you have this enthusiasm, you will find that

your Intuition, that Voice which we are eager
to hear, will become your Master, the one
authority in your lives.

To awaken the interest, you must watch,
you must learn to think, you must learn to
use your imagination, you must learn to suffer
without actually going through all the proc-
esses of ordinary suffering. I will give you
an example. The other day, in my imagination, I went out for a walk with my brother.
We went along a narrow path, and all the
time I was aware that my own shadow was
darker than his. I pondered awhile over this.
I realized that my consciousness was more
centered within myself than in my brother.
It was like looking through two glasses, one
darker than the other, and the darker one was
myself. But I wanted the two shadows to reflect alike; and after a little while the difference disappeared, so that I was able to identify
myself, my personality, with my brother.
And then I lay down in a garden—in imagination—and was looking at a blade of grass.
You know how grass, when it first springs up,
grows absolutely tight in a sheath, and a little
while after it divides into two or three blades.
I felt myself to be that grass which had not

yet divided into separate blades. Then I could feel the grass pushing through from under the earth, the sap rising in it, and the blades separating, and I was myself each blade. When I came back I said to myself: I do not want anything more in my life than to have the capacity to lose the sense of separate self. Because then I am able to forget the "I" and identify myself with the rest of the world—with every kingdom, vegetable, animal, and human! I am then nearer the Truth, nearer that perfection. It is the separate self, it is this narrowing down of the self, this division which self creates that stands in the way.

To have imagination and interest, as I have said, you must keep your mind on the alert, you must watch each other, learn from each other; you must grope till your interest is awakened, till your enthusiasm is clear and defined and not weak and vague, till the flame of genius burns within you. To me the genius is the person who sees his goal, whose enthusiasm is ever alive, who walks steadily toward that goal, who struggles all the time to keep the Vision undimmed; who is never submerged by the petty things of life, by family and worldly troubles, but who is all the time push-

[23]

ing them aside and trying to keep that Vision ever before him clear and pure. Whereas the ordinary man, the bourgeois, is smothered by the world; he does not see the Vision, but succumbs to his environment, and so loses the power over life.

In striving to attain the goal you ought to forget the turmoils of the world, you ought to acquire that interest which drives you ever onwards, gives you vitality, mental and moral. If you are going to create, if you are going to help the world—not just a few, but the whole world—you must get that Vision, fill yourself with that Vision; and when you have filled yourself with it, when you are part of it, when it is your own, when you know the Truth for yourself, then you can bring others to it. That is what you have to do and that is the desire that must be awakened within you; not that you may become gods in your own circles, but that you may give others this Vision that alone matters in life.

The Teacher is for all, He is the world Lover, and He will never be satisfied in giving His knowledge and love to a few. He comes for every one. He longs to awaken the beauty and happiness of life in all, and the more there are of us who understand that attitude, who have something to give, who have struggled, who have lit the candle of genius in ourselves, the better shall we be able to understand, to follow and to serve.

I was speaking about the Buddha and His disciples, and, as I told you, those disciples could not have been ordinary people; they were the exceptions, like the tremendous pine trees in the forest, giving out real love for those who wanted shelter at great heights. Because they understood the great Master, because they breathed the same perfumed air and lived in His world, they were able to give to the world part of that eternal beauty. That is what we have to be: pines on the mountain tops, not the ordinary bushes of the plains, because there are thousands of them; but yet we must be bushes as well. For you can only be a great pine if you know what it is to be a small creeper, or a weed in the garden.

This is what I mean when I say we must take interest in life. We must live every moment of the day. I was reading the Bible yesterday and came to a phrase—"My son, if thou comest to serve God, prepare thy soul for temptation." Your soul, your body, everything, must be alive for temptation of the right kind, so that it gives you delight to serve and to give. That is why you must be cultured. I cannot possibly imagine a real giant being uncultured, uncouth. I do not speak of a giant in body, but of a giant in emotions and in mind.

You can only hear that Voice, its clear tones, its commanding authority, if you have this culture, this interest, this enthusiasm. That is the reason why I always like to urge—though we must pay attention to the physical aspects of life, to beauty, to tidiness, and to well-being—that it is far more important than all these to have emotional and mental culture. You may dress your body as beautifully as you like, but as long as your mind and your emotions are uncivilized you will not be able to hear that Voice. I do not mean that you should not dress nicely, tidily, and really beautifully, but what is of more importance is to get this perfect refinement and sense of culture, both mental and emotional. There is nothing in the world more gratifying, more satisfying, more delightful, than this sense of nobility; and I wish I could give you the interest to acquire that nobility, that insistent demand of your soul. Wherever you are, whether in schools or on platforms or in ordinary life, if you have that attitude of mind, if you have an ear that is striving to hear the Voice, it does not much matter what you are, to what class, what type, what temperament you belong, or what religion you adore. After all, these distinctions and divisions are only marks of the passing world. I do not need anybody to tell me what I am, as long as I know that I am free, happy, straight. I do not need the authority of others. It is those of you who are still uncertain, still striving for the little things of life, that need the authority and blessings of others; thereby setting up a new orthodoxy. As long as you walk with a clear vision, as long as you hear that Voice which is universal, and obey that Voice, it does not matter what any one in the world may say; for you are right when you are obeying the Highest. More and more I want to awaken this desire in you to see for yourself those things that are hidden from your eyes; so that once you have seen, once you have felt, you can go outside and tear the veils from the eyes of others. It is no good merely giving them petty satisfactions,

[27]

little thoughts, and little doctrines. Each one of you has to become such a messenger, such an example. It is much more important than you realize that you should have this craving to see for yourselves, to hear for yourselves, and not be content with what others declare. First you must have the noble craving, then you will satisfy it, and you will expand, and enlarge your souls. Each one of us is the center of his own circle, all the time thinking about himself; but he should think of himself creatively. We should forget, as far as we can, our little selves and feel that we are all one. Though I may have a brown body and black hair, I must be part of you and you must be part of me. For that is the only way to live—to lose ourselves in worlds of others and yet retain our own Vision.

III

PERSONALITY

In trying to realize Truth, the ultimate Happiness, we should bear in mind that the motive must not be personal satisfaction, nor personal enjoyment, but the desire to serve and to help. You should not have the idea that to serve and to help is the lot of the small, the narrow-minded, the bourgeois; that by serving you should become machines, that you should ever obey some one else. In realizing the perfection of Truth, you are gaining real Happiness, and you serve because you cannot help serving.

Be a giver.

I have seen the Vision for myself, and now no one can shatter it or take it away from me, because it is part of my soul, part of my body, part of my very being. It has become unalterable; and the more I change, the more permanent it becomes. You can only see it, you can only absorb the Truth and become part of the Truth, if you learn to become impersonal —in the sense that you lose your own self, your

[29]

own personal point of view, which is small—
and identify yourself with eternal Truth.
Personality, of course, each one of us must
have; you should not get rid of personality,
but you need not be personal. The more you
evolve, the nearer to the Truth you come, the
greater your personality will be and the more
flowerlike your soul will become; but the
further you are from the Truth, the more personal you will be. While you are attaining
this Truth, you will develop your own personality, express your own tendencies.

To gain the impersonal attitude, the first
elementary thing that you have to struggle
against is self-satisfaction. You must revolt
against being satisfied with yourself. If you
succeed in the world, or achieve a spiritual
distinction, there is at once a tendency to be
satisfied with what you have done, and to
glory in it. If you go on submitting yourselves
to that satisfaction, you will not advance, nor
march towards your goal. You cannot get
near to the Truth until you have learned to
be above sorrows and pleasures. You suffer
if you are personal, if you are self-satisfied,
if you are contented with your little selves.
But as long as you keep that Vision constantly

If ego is fulfilled, yes.

[30]

in front of you, as long as you are all the time tearing away the veil you create around it, you can never be self-satisfied. You know how people, when they have succeeded in little things, bear on their faces an appearance of contentment, as though they had done some tremendous work; and gradually that physical satisfaction spreads to the soul, and so they stagnate. If you want to arrive at this goal, if you want to have Truth with you, you must not stop to worship at little shrines and little truths. You need not go and worship at little altars all your lives when the great Temple of worship is there. You are halting, you are wasting your time at these shrines, instead of being driven to worship at the One Altar of Truth ceaselessly, to keep pace with the demands of evolution. And if you believe in the Teacher of Humanity, you are also *beyond* all Altars, dogmas, and doctrines, and see the Truth through all the screens that hide the Vision.

IV

THE TEMPLE OF THE HEART

WE have been talking about the idea of Truth, and how to attain that Truth and that Happiness. I want to impress on you that that Truth, though abstract, is to me the embodiment of my particular Teacher, the embodiment of my Lover.

If you went into a Temple and saw the bare walls and the pillars and nothing but the mere outward shell, it would seem cold and lifeless; for even though there is a certain sense of æsthetic beauty and gorgeousness, in a Temple you also need the image of your creation. Each one of us has a temple, but we must create the Image, the Idol, the Beauty around which we can develop our love and devotion; for if we keep the Temple empty, as most of us do, we cannot create.

It is by adoration, by love, by devotion, that we create, that we make the temple living. And that temple to me is the heart. If you place Him who is the Embodiment of Love and Truth in your heart, if you create Him there with your own hands, your own mind, your own emotions, that heart, instead of being cold and abstract and far away, becomes real and living and radiant. Such is the Truth. And we must realize that this temple, without the vitality, without the life, without the energizing influence that this image gives, becomes hard, becomes cold and joyless. Whereas if you have Him there, you become part of Him, you become Himself. You are the outer temple, and burning inside you is the Eternal, this Holy of Holies into which you can go and worship at your ease, away from the world, away from all the turmoils and all the troubles.

→ But you have to beautify the temple first. You have to make that temple, which is the physical body, perfect, strong, and really beautiful. Every gesture, every movement, every action, whether in time of welfare or in time of sorrow, at every hour, every moment of the day, must be refined and beautiful and must represent the temple in which Eternity abides. Therefore you must have this body absolutely clean, beautiful, radiant, so that He who is in your hearts can show Himself through your physical expressions.

[33]

I do not think you sufficiently realize that with culture of mind and of emotion there takes place refinement of the body. Without culture and refinement the body becomes crude, ugly, and does not represent, in outward expression, Him whom you have within. The first thing you must bear in mind is that to possess Him in your Hearts you must have a suitable tabernacle, a suitable abode. And then with that physical beauty, with that emotional and mental nobility, you will attain serious joyousness.

Most of us, if we become serious lose the sense of joyousness. Seriousness which is without joy, without delight, is artificial in most cases, and so must be avoided. If you cultivate seriousness with joy which springs up because you have Him in your heart, as a part of yourself, then that seriousness takes on a delight instead of turning to morbidity and clumsy expressions. When you see Him you must see Him out of joy and not out of seriousness. You can only approach Him when you are really happy, when you are really enlightened, when you are really delighted; not through the seriousness of religiosity and a gloomy idea of spirituality. When you are really alive with joy, with happiness, He dwells in the Temple of your heart.

Yesterday I went out for a walk by myself, I wanted to regain my original joyousness which for a moment I had lost. I struggled to get to a certain height emotionally and mentally, and I could not get there; I could not attain that altitude, that emotional and mental height, by merely struggling.

I longed to reach my Guru, my Lover, my Genius, my source of Happiness; and, as once before in India, I saw Him, not when I was struggling or trying to get near Him, but when I was natural and there was inside me a bubbling spring of happiness. I saw Him fill the sky, the blades of grass, I saw Him in the whole length of the tree, I saw Him in the pebble, I saw Him everywhere, I saw Him in myself. And so my temple was full, my Holy of Holies was complete. I was He, and He was myself, and that was the Truth for me.

The Truth as an abstract thing is of no value until it gives you that intense personal joy and devotion and the desire to create, not only within yourself, but to create around you. As the birds sing of their own accord, at their

[35]

own ease, of their own full-heartedness, so must Truth come and fill your temple of its own accord; but you must supply the material, you must supply the circumstances, you must supply the marble out of which to carve the image. And that marble must be joy, intense happiness, serious joyousness. Be serious—not with long faces, not grotesquely—but serious with joyousness; have that seriousness which gives you excitement—excitement to play, excitement to be noble, excitement to be happy. And you must create such an image in your hearts. You must make your house His temple.

Every day I have a different Vision of my Truth. When you are on the top of a mountain, there stretches before you a higher range, invisible from the plains. By climbing that range you think you will at last reach the summit whence you will behold all things; but this is not so, for when you have climbed it, there is still another higher range hiding the complete vision. So it is with Truth. There must be constant change, constant alteration of your vision. When you have that desire, that capacity to fill yourself with His genius, with His strength, with His nobility, then you yourself become noble and learn to reflect His divine originality. In Him are all the sources of originality, all the sources of beauty, all the sources of creation; and attempts to be original, beautiful, creative, are of little avail if we have not the understanding and the capacity to touch the source of things. While you have green fields and fair skies and quietness, you should place this graven image in your hearts which you have created out of your own minds, with your own hands.

I desire to force open the doors of the temple in each one of you and let in the sunshine which will help you to destroy that which is ugly, to create anew, and to rebuild; for that is the only way by which you will attain that Truth, the only way you will keep that Eternity in your temple. And when He comes to each one of you, as He so often does come, He will abide with you only if you have the capacity to enshrine Him in the temple of your heart, if you have the wisdom to live with Him, and not lose the fruit of many sorrows and ecstasies.

How joyous and happy you will be if you have the desire to worship at that shrine, at that altar, and forget everything else!

Yesterday, for a moment, I thought I had lost Him, and I could not breathe, I could not move; all the doors and windows of my temple were shut, and I was in darkness. I had to struggle to open them and search for Him. When I found Him and felt the reality of His Presence, then all was once again peace and light and joy. After cloud and rain and storm, there comes a ray of sunshine, all Nature bursts forth to meet that ray. So did I feel yesterday.

Once you realize this beauty, this nobility, this eternal Happiness which comes when you have felt this Truth in your heart, the whole world becomes for you the Holy of Holies. You live and breathe and look from there, and every little thing, every little action, every little thought, falls into its proper place; and you get the true refinement, the true restraint, the true enlightenment. That is the only way you will acquire the spark of genius, that is the only way you will be happy. If you have this serious joyousness, the sense of well-being, spiritual, moral, and intellectual, then you will see the glory; and every one of you will have that light, that purity, that sense of nobility and greatness which nothing in the world can disturb. Everything breathes His glory, and all that which is ignoble withers away and dies. You can have no conception of your loss if you do not go to the source of things. Only at the source will you know the Beginning and the End. And, what is much more important—you will be there with Him, you will be a part of Him; and thus you yourself will become the source for thousands of others.

So I want you to keep before you this idea of a temple and of the image within. Wherever you are, whether you are in a room or in a street, whether you are playing or at work —you will be unruffled and have that solemn poise, for He is always with you. What does it matter to the God within if there is strife or struggle outside the temple? As long as you are tranquil, as long as you are worshiping and encouraging others to worship, as long as you are making others happy, what does anything else matter? All forms of outward worship, all interpreters of God, cease to affect you. As long as you have that glory you will be happy; when you have drunk at that source you will be a genius, you will create, you will make others happy. And for that we exist.

V

THE RIVER AND THE OCEAN

ON a day when there is mile upon mile of blue sky and there are innumerable shadows, the only thing to talk about is the Kingdom of Happiness; and of how, while we have the physical attractions and the physical beauty all around us, we may also have the spiritual Happiness, that Kingdom of Happiness, within us. The only possible way to possess that Kingdom is to forget yourselves and to identify your souls with the Eternal. We all have this intense belief—to some it is more than belief —that a time must come, as I think it will come, when that Voice to which we have been listening, that Voice whose command we have obeyed, will urge us to give up all and follow Him. That is going to happen to each one of us; that order, that command, will come to each one, in varied forms, under different aspects, under different conditions, but it is bound to come. And when it comes, in what attitude of mind, in what emotional condition, shall we respond? How shall we give up and follow? What will it mean to us?

I have thought out for myself what it will involve. To me it seems that to give up the physical—the ordinary physical comforts, physical well-being, wealth, family relations —will be comparatively easy; what will be much more difficult and much more serious and much more worth giving up, much more sacred and holy, will be to give up my separate self, and identify myself with Him. Identifying yourself with Him means that you must set aside your own predilections, your own prejudices, your own particular inclinations, and all such things. That is much more difficult, and yet that is what you will have to do. You will have to forget what you are and become like Him.

Have you ever noticed how a small hill will hide a whole range of snowy mountains, so that you think that that little hill is the whole view and forget the tremendous vista stretching far away—mile upon mile behind it? It it exactly the same with us. We think that by giving up little things we have succeeded. Little things do not matter; we need not give up the little things; it is like standing in front of the little hill—we must go beyond that little hill to see the giant peaks. It is no good clinging to your own particular line, your own particular attitude, your own particular form of devotion or worship. The stars sparkle, brilliant and beautiful, before the moon comes out, and then they all give way, and go into the background, before the one queen, the one ruler of the sky. So must you all before Him who is our Ruler. It does not mean that you must throw away your individuality, but that you must become like Him; and you can only do that if you are able to look at everything in life from His point of view.

To an artist who looks at a cloud or the skies or a tree, these have a different meaning; he looks at them from the point of view of how he will paint them, of how he can reproduce them as a symbol to the world—not necessarily by copying them, but by sharing with others what he has perceived in them. That is exactly what you have to do. You have to destroy all the things that bind you and climb to that altitude where you become a part of Him; and from there you should look at yourself and at the world. It is no good always surrounding yourself with particular delights of your own. You must go up to that height and from there direct your minds and emotions and physical bodies, and that is the only way in which you will be able to follow Him.

How many of you, I wonder, will really understand, really follow, when the moment actually comes, the moment when you hear that Voice which you recognize as the absolute authority, whose command is final? I wonder how many of you, even though you may obey, will mingle yourselves with Him as a drop of water that disappears in the sea, a river that flows into the vast ocean? You are all much too narrowly individualistic, you have your own particular God, your own particular delight, your own particular way of speech, way of thought, way of expression. To follow, does not mean that you should blindly accept; but to follow means that you must keep your eyes open and your hearts clear, free from all prejudices, all preconceived ideas, and so be able to lose yourselves in the Eternal. That is the only way in which you should follow, the only way in which you can possibly create. If you live in that Eternity, at that stupendous height, you become a genius, you become that which each one of you really longs to be, and then you will be happy.

It is in forgetting the separate self, in destroying that self, in mingling with the Universe, that you can find Happiness; and when you make distinctions by talking about particular groups, particular temperaments, particular types, you are wandering away from reality, not realizing that these are but marks of distinction, mere indications of your special environment. They do not solve the problem; the only solution is in the forgetting of the separate self, in becoming part of the Eternal.

Follow the Eternal which is perpetual, immutable, not the fleeting and the momentary. You will obtain a true perspective of your purpose, if you realize that you must give suitable opportunities on the physical for the education of the soul. We always talk about educating the physical, but forget the education of the super-physical. The ego desires to evolve and attain perfection; and here on the physical, if you have in view the longing of the soul, you, the lower mind, will realize when and how you must yield to the cravings of the greater Self.

You ought to develop that habit of living in the Kingdom of Happiness, because I do not think you sufficiently realize how expansive it it, how this Kingdom stretches mile after mile if you once enter its borders. I do not think you understand that Happiness, real Happiness, is above all things in the world, physical or spiritual. It is the only state worth entering, the only Kingdom worth conquering and possessing. And I would take you all into that Kingdom and let you see the beauty of it for yourselves, because once you have seen it you will not abandon it, you will no longer desire the transient, changeable things. I am sure that more and more, as time goes on, it will be borne in on you that this is the only Truth worth having, the only Truth worth giving. → You must also have culture, the culture which comes from reading, the culture of the ordinary attainments in the physical, the culture of consideration, of happiness, of that intense, serious joyousness. If you can have the culture from all these things, imbibe it, make it a part of your nature; you will then become His real followers. Without culture, without refinement, you cannot become part of the more refined and the more cultured, which is He; nor can you stand with Him and coöperate intelligently and enthusiastically with Him. A man who is an artist, who is creating,

[45]

who is suffering, who stumbles, will be nearer to Him than the one who is merely satisfied and worships at his own particular altar.

You must be such an artist, and coöperate with Him, and give to the world what each one of you really understands. And when you are in that state you have no idea how the sense of loneliness, the sense of depression, all those things which hinder us, which kill our spirit, which weaken our sense of well-being, disappear. When you are part of that one Kingdom that matters in life, when you are with that Life that lasts through ages and æons, you forget whether you are lonely, whether you are depressed, whether you are great or successful. What most of you fear is loneliness, lack of love and personal friendship for each other. Those things, though they are pleasant for the moment, though they have their value, you do not miss, because you have companionship with the Eternal. Every tree, every bird, every blade of grass, every shadow, gives you something which is worth more than the passing physical satisfactions, for it is part of the Eternal. That is why you must have your life centered there, and thus gain your outlook from the Eternal.

VI

THE VALUE OF EXPERIENCE

I WANT to talk about that Voice, that Tyrant, that you must train, and whose authority is the only command you must obey. As you begin to evolve, you will naturally meet problems, come against difficulties, which must be solved by yourself. You have to become like a tree which stands innumerable storms and knows its own strength, its own delight in the protection it gives, and which nothing in the world, no wind, earthly or heavenly, can uproot; it is as firm as a rock. As you see a rock remaining unmoved, although the waves of the ocean dash around it, so do you see this tree standing firm, giving shelter to thousands of birds, because it is well rooted, deeply grown. That is what you have to be.

The only authority you recognize, the only command you allow, must be the Voice of that Intuition which is unalterable, which nothing in the world can shake. In this way you

[47]

gradually develop that sense of beauty which is of your own creation, which increases as time goes on and gives you joy; that is the only authority that any civilized, cultured, and spiritual person can recognize; not the authority of another, not the spiritual label of another, for you can only recognize that which you feel from within.

We have been discussing how to develop that Voice, that unyielding Tyrant, and we have examined one or two ideas. I want to put before you another idea. If you desire to recognize such a Voice, you must have revolution, you must have anarchy *within* you, you must have discontentment; you must be in a whirlpool, mentally and emotionally, and the center of the whirlpool must become stronger and stronger, so that the little things of life are thrown out, and only the strength of purpose remains. Out of the chaos within you, you must give birth to the dancing start! That discontentment which gives birth to true contentment must be encouraged, and not set aside and subjugated and killed out. The more you question and demand, the greater will be the strength of your whirlpool, the greater the shattering, the greater the strength of your desire to discover the Truth. You have to create a whirlpool in your mind and in your emotions; not a whirlpool of mere sentimentality and excitement, but a whirlpool that forces aside and destroys the unimportant—a whirlpool that centers round a single purpose; and it whirls round and round with greater speed and gathers greater energy, and out of that energy the true genius, the dancing star of your creation, will be born.

How are you going to gain this divine, discontentment? You cannot acquire this discontentment by merely listening to others; they can but provide the scaffolding which helps you to climb and to build, but you must carry your own bricks and your own mortar, you must yourself be the builder. For this, you must go through your own experiences, and that is why mere innocence is not spiritual. The man who knows great sorrows, great ecstasies, great devotion, great bursts of adoration or of anger, can become a truly spiritual person, because he is all the time seeking, all the time asking.

In order to become spiritual, to live happily, and to serve, you must have a "soul prepared for temptation."

[49]

Experience is essential. People who are childishly innocent tend to be petty and narrow and jealous, and it is against such trivial things that we must fight. These do not tend to give great and true experiences. You do not want the innocency of a child who has had no experience, who does not know what it is to suffer, what it is to be in a turmoil of emotion, what it is to suffer mentally; a child but prattles, and uses pretty words and babbles. You must be like the man who has suffered, who knows, who has built. Such a man you must be. You must have your own thrill of life, and not the thrill of another. Nor does it mean that you must rush into absurd experiences, absurd expressions of your feelings. Ordinary pleasures, pains, sorrows, and joys must be your experiences; out of these you must build. They are your channels, your rivers on which you must sail to the vast ocean where you lose your own experience, your own identity, and become a drop in that ocean. But you must have vessels in which you can go; you must be able to sail, you must be able to row, you must have all the accumulation of experiences behind you; you must be thrilled at the idea of new experiences of the right kind; you must have this divine discontent, this chaos, which shall give birth to the dancing star.

Most people are self-satisfied, and contented with their own little lives—and thereby create for themselves the narrow world of mediocrity. And if you would be different, you must find yourself, give birth to your true self, follow your own path, keep in view your own goal—the goal which is Happiness, which is Truth. Like a fisherman, who goes from pond to pond, from river to river, from ocean to ocean, fishing, gathering experience, not being satisfied with one little fish, or with one enormous fish, you must desire to gather and keep the various types, colors, and expressions of divinity, in all the oceans of life. You must hear for yourselves that call, that Voice which only comes through experience, through thought, through feeling. You do not want pictures, you do not want ceremonies, you do not want anything in life if you have this one thing, this adventurous, divine longing. In the bird as it flies in the blue sky, the shimmer of light on its wing, in the solitary tree, the quiet meadows and the little stream that wanders by, in the flower, there dwells divinity;

[51]

they are the truth of life, they are the real expressions of spirituality. Because when you recognize Truth in those little things of everyday life and lose yourself in their beauty, you will have acquired that eternal Truth, you will then live in that Kingdom of Happiness. When you have acquired this, you will be able to give it to others. The person who has it not and who yet is trying to convince others, is the hypocrite; but the person who has it, in however small a degree, will speak with certainty, with knowledge, with authority. You will speak with authority because you know what it means to feel with the Universe and with humanity, with all who suffer, with all who are happy; you will create and make others create their own ideas, their own conceptions of life. That will give a different tone to your existence, a different joy, a different thrill; then all the outward forms and expressions will have no value, because you are at the Eternal source of all things. And you can only get there if you have this chaos, this discontentment, this perpetual longing. One vision of the Eternal does not satisfy; one vision opens up another, and so it goes on through life after life. Evolution does not suddenly begin at a certain moment, nor stop in a given moment, nor after one life; it is an endless road, and the person who enjoys walking does not stop to worship at little shrines, small conventionalities, outward forms and altars of supposed greatness—otherwise evolution becomes a long-drawn suffering. If he sees in the distance the temple of his own creation, the image of his own making, which he has created through suffering, through happiness, through the beauty of life, then he is walking perpetually in the Kingdom of Happiness.

You must be either one thing or the other; either you must be a genius, a creator, a destroyer, or an ordinary weed in the middle of the stream that is buffeted about from side to side. You must be the main current of life, the main force of life, because you live in Him and have your being in Him. The beauty which is Truth, which, in its turn, is He whom you all long for, He whom you adore, He whose image you create in your hearts, becomes a part of you, because you have striven towards Him and have found Him. Such a conception gives the inspiration to exist, the inspiration to breathe, to think, and to feel.

But if you are contented and self-satisfied, you lose the great adventurous thrill of spirituality; instead of helping, you become mere followers; instead of being creators, you are mere waste products of life.

I wish you could see—I am sure you do, for every one of us sees in moments of ecstasy and happiness—the importance of maintaining this standard, this culture, and of living in this Kingdom of Happiness. If you are there, dwelling safely in that Kingdom, you can wander forth and create more vitally, more dangerously, more nobly, than any one else, because you can always withdraw into that Kingdom. It gives you a sense of thrill, of vitality, of being great not only for yourself, but in helping others and in destroying things which do not matter and in creating the things which are Eternal. Instead of being giants of ignorance you must be creative giants. At the present time we are all seeking, groping, questioning, while the solution of all these things lies under every common stone, in all things that live and move, in all things animate and inanimate. If you are really enlightened, you can go out and become messengers of that Kingdom. I have drunk at

[54]

the source, and I long to bring every one of you to it; and when you have delighted and sported in the shades of Eternity, you will want to bring others to it also.

VII

IN THE COMPANY OF GREAT MEN

I WANT again to impress upon you that taking interest in the excellency of the Kingdom of Happiness is of the utmost importance. One can see by your words, by the way you talk, whether you are living in that Kingdom or not. I have watched you and myself to see whether we live continuously in that Kingdom. By our attitude, and by the conduct of our life, and by the desires that surge up, we can judge and discover how far away we are from that abode of reality, or how far within it we live.

If you are striving to live in that Kingdom, you conquer with ease your special troubles, you forget your special burdens, your special peculiarities, and you adopt the sorrows and sufferings of the world. When you live in that Kingdom you cannot separate yourself from your daily actions; in your thought, in your work, in everything that you do, you are living in that Kingdom, hence you translate that Kingdom into your own actions.

You can see how different are those people who have caught even a fleeting glimpse of that Kingdom; how happy, how really balanced, neither too emotional nor too intellectual. You can see by their attitude, by their whole atmosphere, that they know what it means to live in that Kingdom. It would be a thousand pities if we lived there only at rare moments, only when we are meditating, only when we are alone. You can only live in that Kingdom—if your whole being throbs with happiness. You must express this happiness in all your feelings, in all the things that you do daily; not just live in that Kingdom for a few brief moments like a little insect, and then vanish for the rest of the day, to be born again on the morrow. This is what most of you are doing—a word will betray the whole of your mind, the whole trend of your outlook. I feel it is so important, that you be really serious and joyous, instead of struggling in vain and making vast useless efforts. You must not have the idea that some privileged people alone are in that Kingdom and the rest are not; as long as there is any one who is struggling, who has nobility of thought and emotion, be assured that he is living in that Kingdom.

We must transform this center at Eerde, and the world at large, into a veritable Kingdom of Happiness, and you must help because you are living in it, because you are creating it, and you must give your capacities, your sufferings, your happiness and pleasures and joys; you must give the material with which we can build—every one of you must help, not one individual alone. That is why you must be great, that is why you must live and breathe only in that Kingdom of Happiness. Every barrier, all pettiness in our outlook, must be destroyed. You do not know how thrilling it is and how pleasurable and how exciting—it is much more so than any cinema performance, than any game in the world.

Imagine for a moment that we are all gods; then we could all sit around a table with Him. Think what we could do, think what it would mean, if we were like the Buddha and His disciples. He was a super-genius, the greatest of humans, and His disciples were also geniuses, they were the great men of their day. And you can imagine the delicious air, the atmosphere which those men, those gods, must have created. Then go to the other extreme, and think of all the personifications of Evil in the world—think of the time they would have! They would be attempting to annihilate and confuse the work of the gods. Whereas it is those like us who are between the two extremes, who form the major portion of the world. When you have a precious vase or jewel, you must find a safe in which you can guard it. And when He comes, as He does come; when He is with us, as He is with us; we must be the great men, and each one of us must struggle to reach the height of perfection. And then if we are gathered together, you can imagine the intense delight of that association; for we shall be companions with nobility, with great artists, great creators, with the divinity that is well-balanced in perfect physical bodies. There is nothing more wonderful in the world than living with great men, with great ideas, with men who are the principles themselves and not merely the outward shell of some inner reality.

It is the person who has not tasted happiness, who has not suffered, who has not had many experiences, that cannot be companion with great men nor even with great sinners.

Such an individual can never help, neither can he give nor enjoy that happiness which is lasting. Such an individual can never know the difference between the beautiful, the refined, and the coarse, the vulgar, and where judgment has no value. For he is neither a creator nor a destroyer; he is merely carried along by the whims and fancies of the world of mediocrity.

Because you desire not to belong to this world of mediocrity, you must bear in mind that all that you think and feel matters vitally. For this reason you must develop a fine physical body, with refined emotions and a cultured mind. Because if you have not a perfect body, mind, and emotions, you will disfigure the beauty and disturb the harmony of the whole company of great men; you might be wise in your words, but your outward expression, your personality, betrays your inner development which is not perfect.

You must also have perfect cleanliness, perfect health; and you can see the importance of this, you can see why you must have clean and healthy bodies, why you must take care of them, as you take care of a most precious jewel. It is the same with your emotions and your thoughts. Ugly thoughts and ugly feelings, though you may not expose them outwardly to your friends or your neighbors, yet they will betray themselves in your looks, in your sayings, in your attitude, in your outlook on life. I interest myself very often in looking at people's faces, their gestures, their general deportment; and I can usually distinguish the type to which each one belongs. I know these superficial things may be deceptive, that one cannot always judge truly, but they generally betray the inner character. You must therefore perfect the body, the emotions, and the mind, before you can attain and live eternally in that Kingdom of Happiness.

You must not conform without reason, without understanding, and fit yourself into molds. Can you imagine the sea, that mass of animation and turmoil, ever fitting into a form? It will break all forms, nothing can hold it, nothing can bind it. We all want to fit into forms because it is so much easier, so much more comfortable, means so much less struggle. To those who are not enslaved by forms, who are living in this Happiness, in this Kingdom that has no boundaries, to them the thing of value, the thing of beauty, is this boundless, limitless expanse. You must realize that if you would really live in the presence of great men, you must develop an outlook which cannot be bound, which cannot be limited. You will realize in what great ecstasy you can live—in what balanced ecstasy—if you constantly imagine that you are always living in that Kingdom and that you are with great men. How many of you are capable of being with a great man, with a great genius, with Him who is the embodiment of this Kingdom of Happiness? Very, very few indeed. And you can see the anguish, the pain it must cause to such a person that there should be only two or three companions, instead of the entire world with Him, working with Him, delighting with Him.

I want also to talk about affection, because I do not think you realize what force, what vitality, true affection, well-balanced affection, gives. I am using the word balanced, because you generally find that those who possess tremendous feelings of affection are without strength, without control, without poise. These feelings are like water, which, if poured out too freely, inundates and overflows, and has no lasting effect. That is why you must have balance. If you have well-balanced affection—not sentimentality, not mere gush—but that eternal thing which we call love, then you begin to lose the separate self. Each one of you must have felt that affection which bubbles, which expands, which is ever growing; and it becomes wider and wider, so that you feel this love not only for a special few, but for the whole neighborhood. Such an affection makes you forget, annihilate, that self which is the root of all sorrow. That is why a person who has not that immense love, becomes personal, talks, interferes, gossips, does all those small things which a great man, a real god, would not dream of doing. The moment you forget yourself, the self which is in each one of you, and identify that with the Great Self of the world, then you are living in that Kingdom, then you want to bring the whole world to live with you.

At present it may be said about each one of you that you are making a feverish attempt, rather than that you have accomplished a deed. You are still struggling and struggling, but you have not attained. You do not risk, you do not dare, and you do not plunge into the ocean; but you are like the child at the sea, who hesitatingly puts a foot into the water and draws it back immediately at the first chilling touch of the cold sea. If you slip, never mind—you will rise up again; if you swim, you will get there. But you must not hesitate all day long as to whether you should attempt to reach the further shore; you must take the plunge because your Voice urges you. And if you do not hear that Voice, you should be metaphorically sore all the day; you should have not a single moment of peace, of tranquillity, of happiness, if that Voice does not urge you onwards. You should go towards the source of things; and when once you reach that source, you become the god, the superman, the master.

The Buddha, the Christ, and other great Teachers of the world, went to the source of life. They became the Master Artists. Once knowing the nature and the supreme greatness of the Source, They became Themselves that Source, the Path, and the Embodiment of Wisdom and Love. This should be our purpose. You cannot all be the Buddha or the Christ, but you can all have the same dreams, the longings, the desires, the aspirations.

When once you have realized the glory of Their Kingdom, then you can work out for yourself along what particular line of creation you will express your vision of that eternal glory. Then you will be the greatest of writers, or the greatest of artists, or the greatest of scientists; then you will have the tongue of the learned. There lies the thrill of spirituality, the only ambition in the world that it is worth while possessing. You must be independent—not only emotionally and intellectually—but also of all physical entanglements. This is the only way to attain the greatest happiness—by gaining complete liberty in thought, in emotions, and in all things physical. This is the only way to live in the Kingdom of Happiness.

VIII

MIND, THE CREATOR

MIND is the essence of divinity; but it is quite obvious that mind can either create or destroy, that it controls and guides the emotion—the impetus that drive us on to our goal. The mind can and must find for itself the Truth, and must learn to live for itself, in that Kingdom of Happiness; without a trained mind and a native intelligence, you cannot come near to your goal. You can also see that it is the mind that makes things narrow, that longs for forms, that desires to fill those forms. It is the mind that always tends to be concrete; and against that characteristic of the mind you must guard yourselves.

We often feel that what we do is right, that our particular path is the only path, that our particular temple, our particular altar, our particular ceremony, our particular form of worship, and our particular creation of the outward form, can alone be the true one; and that through that channel alone can the Divine express Himself in outward life. We say in effect: You are wrong, but if you follow me, if you do as I do, think as I think, then you will be right. That is what you are all thinking. That is the real stumbling block for each one of you who is attempting to enter the Kingdom. For here, there is no such narrow uniformity; here any one who is struggling, who is living a noble life, who is really beautiful by nature, in mind and in emotion, can be one with all and *is* one with all. The sense of unity is what matters most in life; that is the only food you can give to the hungry, the only solution to all the problems of life. The intolerant idea that you must be wrong if you are independent, but right if you follow me —my special intuition, my special Master, my special Deity—is contrary to spiritual progress. As long as there is enthusiasm, the spark of divine discontent, the longing for happiness, the longing to escape from the Maya of life, it does not matter if you belong to any religion or to none, to any sect, class, color, or to any faith. Because then you are on the true road leading to that Kingdom. This is the only idea you must bear in mind always.

You can only enter this Kingdom if you are living a noble life, and you can only become a

[*67*]

citizen of that Kingdom if you are struggling against narrowness, against the spirit of exclusion. It is for this purpose you must have a mind that is clear and clean and includes all things; because, if you have such a mind, you will have equally noble, happy emotions; whereas if you are exclusive and desirous to shut out every one else because you think you are different—which is but the assertion of self —then you shall not enter into the Kingdom of Happiness.

If you know that some person is suffering, if you know that he is going through difficult times, that he is not happy within himself, that he is struggling, the only shade under which he can rest, the only comfort that you can give, is this Happiness that you have tasted, this delight that you have experienced in finding the things which are eternal. I wish I could give you this Happiness so that you, in your turn, could give it to others, could make others feel its immense reality; I wish I could lead you to that Kingdom of Happiness, because only when you have entered that Kingdom, have lived in that domain, can you feed the hungry, appease the suffering, and give balm to the wounded soul.

[68]

You must live there your own life, obey your own Voice, find your own Master, your own breath of life. This is the only ambition worth having. Then you can be of the world and give to the world, because you are full, because your soul and your body, your whole mind and emotions, are full of that Eternity; and you can give without the least hesitation, without holding back at all. The more you grow, the more you must cultivate this spirit. You cannot be happy until you make others happy, and you can only make others happy if you have entered that Kingdom, if you have obeyed, if you have caught the whisper of that Voice which is Eternal. In that way only you can lead people, in that way only you can give them happiness, and encourage the struggle after nobility, encourage them to listen to their own murmurings of Divinity. In struggling they will suffer, but all suffering, all struggles, are part of the process towards the deed accomplished, and that deed is the finding of Happiness. This is the true breath from the mountains, that makes you intoxicated with Eternity, that gives you the immense strength to stand alone.

The tree on the summit of a mountain must

naturally be much stronger than a tree in the plains—it must be, because it gets all the breezes of the world, its roots are deeper because it must withstand mighty winds; it must be much more dignified, much more noble, because it is nearer heaven; it catches the first rays of the dawn, it is nearer the stars. It should be exactly the same with you if you would enter into that region of absoluteness; you must have deeper roots, because you are nearer to the Gods, and deeper agonies of growth, because you see the first rays of the sun. And when you are at that height you will realize the illusion, the Maya, the uselessness, of the things which are not lasting, which are not perpetual. The idea of such a solitary tree, always living in the fresh air of the mountains, getting stronger and stronger day by day, which can only fall when the mountain ceases to stand—such an idea as this gives me strength.

That is the spirit which He will give us, that is the spirit which we must possess to understand Him, that is the only Happiness, the only conviction worth having, that is the only way by which we can hold Him in our hearts, that is the only way in which we can

[70]

follow Him; because we do not think and feel we are different, because we do not belong to narrow sects, because we have drunk at the fountain of reality, because we have been there and have the capacity to reach the heavens, we desire all others to come and taste the same lasting happiness.

This is the only Truth which anyone who is intelligent, who is happy, or who is suffering, can accept and must accept; if you can only have that personal knowledge, you will become like the tree which lasts through eternity, under whose shelter men can rest, a tree which only grows in that Kingdom.

You must grow wings, new wings every day, to fly to that height; and you can only grow new wings if you are all the time soaring, expanding, growing, struggling. That means you must change every day; you must throw off all those things which clog, which bind, which restrain, which do not give you absolute freedom, which bind you to the illusions of life. That is the only way to grow, to have fresh energies, fresh delights. And only with new wings can you soar into the heights.

You must be falling in love all the time.

Everything that lives, everything that moves or does not move, should give you a fresh impetus to love more; as you desire every one to dwell in that Kingdom, you want to bring everything around you into that Kingdom. And when every one of you can spread this Kingdom of Happiness, you will then realize that outward forms have no intrinsic importance, and that your only real value lies in bringing others into that Kingdom. That is why I wish that I could give you a part— or the whole—of that Happiness which I have found. Having once tasted this I can taste it again, having once realized this I can always realize it again; but the person who has not tasted it, who does not know the richness of it, the beauty of it, can never realize the fullness and the glory of life. When once he has tasted this, he will never be satisfied with transient things. That is why I want to give you, that is why I should like to make you taste, make you breathe, my Happiness—make you live in my Kingdom.

For this reason you must wake up, you must open all the windows and all the doors of your souls and issue forth in search of the one reality in life; you must not lose yourselves in feverish and vain attempts, in corridors, in darkened alleys, but must seek out the places of light, the abode of Truth, the Kingdom of Happiness, and there each one of you must dwell.

In that state of ecstasy, of tremendous joyousness, having lost the one thing that keeps you down, the self, you find the only source of inspiration, the only beauty that you need, and the only truth worth clinging to, worth possessing, worth struggling for, worth sacrificing everything to attain. You must have that ambition—I cannot find a better word for it—you must have that intense desire to enter that Kingdom; and then whatever your actions may be, they will bear the mark of Eternity, and wherever you may be, you are the emblem of that Kingdom.

IX

THE ALTAR OF THE WORLD

IT must be quite clear to all of you that the only goal that we should have is the attainment of the inward conviction of a Truth that cannot be shaken or doubted. This Truth cannot be imposed upon you; you must attain it for yourself, and you can only arrive at it if you awaken and listen to that inner Voice. All action, all thought, all ideas, must originate from the Truth which you have discovered and understood for yourself. Such Truth cannot be shared, cannot be handed over to another. Every great Teacher has insisted upon this fact, that you must find the Truth for yourself; and that after having understood it, you must live according to that Truth. Then you are yourself the embodiment of that Truth, as well as the preacher, the signpost on the road to eternal Happiness.

To understand this idea, you must live according to its edicts, you must have desires that are worthy of the Truth. You must have the impetus to grow in your natural environment, as a flower grows, beautifully and naturally; and while it is in the stage of the bud, it surely knows its fulfillment—that one day it will see the sunshine, that it will give forth scent to the world. So must each one of you, during that period of growth, think and meditate on that light and truth which will come the moment you are fully blossomed.

You can have that sunshine, that energy, that delight, only if you listen to that Voice, and not blindly accept the authority, the tradition, of another. These must be set aside; in other words you must be a lawgiver unto yourself; you must live according to your own ideas, your own intuitions, which are the outcome of experiences in this and other lives. There is only one Law, only one Nirvana, only one Kingdom of Happiness, only one essence; and if you understand this thoroughly, you will act on this understanding. The more you develop, the more you think, the more you suffer, the nearer you should get to that essence, to that Oneness, to that eternal Truth. You are bound to have these doubts, questionings, and a great turmoil within, until you hear for yourself, grasp for yourself, this Truth.

While we are trying to understand, we must have the conscience, not of fools but of wise men; we should have the conscience of those who have seen the Vision of the nobler side of life, and not of small and ignorant people with their ideas and conceptions. And if you would escape from this little conscience, these weak whisperings of that Voice, you must thoroughly understand what the Kingdom of Happiness means, what the Law means, what the Truth means.

As the rain falls on the earth and nourishes every kind of tree, every species of plant and every flower, so does this one essence run through everything without variance. The hands of the potter mold clay and give shape to vessels useful and beautiful, some to hold flowers, rice, curds; others are vessels of impurity. But all these are made by the same hands, made of the same clay, are the product of the same wheel which whirls round and round. In essence we are the same, but in the world of form we are different; and according to that difference does our understanding of the Truth vary. The bigger you are, the more you have suffered, the more you have enjoyed, the nearer you are to the oneness of this essence. This is the only Law, the only aim that can guide you to the Kingdom of Happiness. It is the recognition of the same essence in things, all different in outward form, and living in the light of this knowledge, that can alone bring lasting happiness.

It takes some time to have such a realization; and to understand the Truth you must train your will, you must use your mind, because it is the will, the mind, which guides. It can guide you along the right path or the wrong path; it can guide you away from personality, away from prejudices, away from all the petty little things which make you separate, or it can make you cling to the thought that you are different from others. If you have the mind that discriminates, which has learned through many experiences and sacrifices to distinguish between the real and the unreal, the permanent and the transient, you can then be guided by that one Law, you can then walk along that one solitary path. Then you cease to make useless experiments, because you have learned to sacrifice everything for this one Happiness. You must learn to sacrifice yourself, your predilections, your preju-

dices, your narrow selfish affections, your
worldly bonds, in order to walk on this path
that leads to happiness.

You do not tread that path because of my
assurance, nor because of the labels that I may
offer you, nor because you take shelter under
the authority of another. You tread it because it is your own desire, your own longing,
your own wish to search out the Truth. You
grow as the flower grows, naturally, beautifully, because it is in its own nature to unfold
and to be happy. You can only find the
Truth if you use your will, the will that you
have trained, that you have carefully watched
and guided, that you have fed with proper
nourishment; and until you have such a will,
you will find that, instead of succeeding, instead of deeds accomplished, you are still but
making feverish attempts; instead of sur-
mounting, you are still creating barriers; instead of shouting from the mountain tops,
you are still crying in the valleys.

Every one in the world must recognize that
there is but one Law, one Aim, one Truth,
one Kingdom of Happiness; and that you can
enter it only if you live according to that Law,
which is the recognition of the oneness of life,

of the one essence in all things. Such a conception—at least for me—gives a tremendous sense that nothing really matters; it gives me a sense of absolute certainty, which certainty brings a sense of absolute peace within, which cannot be shaken, which cannot be taken away by anybody else, which cannot be thrown down by my passing unhappiness, passing suffering, which cannot cease because I lose the affection of another or the estimation of the crowd; because it is my own flower, my own creation, my own treasure, which nobody in the world can take away. When once you have this peace you have power, you can do what you want. You can remain on the mountain top, whether you are alone or surrounded by all the world, because you have gone through the experiences, the sufferings, the pleasures and the joys; and when once you have this peace, this power, you become real, and wherever you may be you are all the time living in that Kingdom.

Have you ever seen in a power station gigantic dynamos generating electricity, and the great wheels? They are comparatively silent, but yet you know that all the time they are generating energy, immense power. You must be such a dynamo of power, dignified and balanced; and you will be that only if you realize that one essence of life, that unity, and escape from this Maya, this unreality.

Thus you obtain purposefulness without which none of us can be happy, none of us can evolve. You must have purpose in life, interest in life. Most of us live in a house of many barriers, indifferent whether we go forth to see the source of light or remain satisfied by its mere reflection. If you have this purpose, it gives you determination, it gives you will; and you arrive at your goal. Having found yourself, nobody can thwart you, nobody can put you aside, nobody can create barriers; and having arrived by yourself at your destination, your altar, your temple, whether there be other worshipers or not, you can worship with greater glory, with greater enthusiasm.

Once you have cultivated these capacities, you will find that other qualities, equally important for the understanding of life, will naturally assert themselves. Patience, which gives you a sense of mental well-being; restraint and poise, so necessary for the outward expression of your understanding of the

Truth; and coöperative independence. You must be independent; you must be free; mentally and emotionally and physically; and yet learn to coöperate, because we are all walking along the same path, to the same goal, obeying the same Law and the same Voice. When once you have recognized this Law which is universal, the one Life in all things, then you will live with true friendliness and affection for all.

Only then is it possible to realize the happiness or the sorrows of others.

Those of us who are seeking this Kingdom must not be bound by traditions, old or recent, but must live a new life because we have understood the purpose of life. Those who come here,* who come here to live and work, who come here to learn to suffer, if they have not suffered before, who come here to seek the pleasures, the happiness of Divinity, must be inspired by this one Law, must all enter this one Kingdom of Happiness. We must be inspired by the same hope, the same freshness —though we may have clouds, though we may be shut out for the moment from the sun. This place must give forth a new creative

* Eerde, Omnen, Holland.

[81]

energy, new ideas of life, ancient and forgotten solutions of our modern problems, a purer breath of life whose fragrance shall intoxicate the world.

You must all enter into that Kingdom of Happiness and drink at the same source and worship at the same altar, because He whom we worship is our altar, because He is the Source of all things. He is above arguments, above discussions, above personal ambitions, above personal struggles; He is our self. As long as you recognize that Law, and as long as you are struggling, and there is nobility in that struggle, you will then bring a new understanding to life, a new impetus and happiness to those who are in sorrow. That is why you must come here—to gain strength to build, to still the wounds of your life; and the moment they are stilled, the moment you are pacified, the moment you have that peace, you can give it to others.

This is not the place to seek new labels, to satisfy personal vanities; this must be the place where each should live as dangerously as he can, as forcefully as he can, as adventurously as he can, according to this eternal Law. You must not make of this place a wilderness of false ideals, or yourselves into tame beings; you must not create little gods and worship at little shrines—this you can do elsewhere, this is not what is wanted here; this is the wrong kind of worship, the wrong kind of attitude, the wrong kind of devotion. When once you have drunk at this source, you do not want to drink anywhere else; when once you have worshiped here, you do not want to worship anything else in the world. Who wants to worship by the light of one candle, when he can have the sun? But that is just what you are doing all day long—justifying the small worship, in small houses, in small cells. Here we are trying to build the greater altar where all humanity can worship.

I feel more and more that you must find this for yourself. It must be a part of you. I can preach, I can talk, I can shout, I can feel, I can feel the thrill of happiness of this Kingdom for myself—perhaps I can kindle a little enthusiasm in you; but you must make the effort. You must have the true and lasting ambition, the ambition to arrive at your goal, to enter this Kingdom of Happiness, where there is beauty which gives real joy, where there is the only Truth worth seeking, where there

[83]

is the Law by which alone you can live. You must be free to grow, free to feel, free to strive. It is no good my drinking and my eating to keep you healthy. In that way the world could be saved to-morrow. I could fill myself with all the best foods in the world; but it is you who must nourish your own soul, must give the proper conditions, the proper environment, the proper adventures to that soul to enable it to advance, to live greatly. Each one of you must find, if you have not already found, your own Voice, your own ray of the sun; you must have this turmoil, this longing and this ambition. When you have found it, I assure you, whether you are living in a castle, or whether you are going naked with a begging bowl, it will make no difference, because you will have found the one thing by which you can live forever; and then only will you be able to make others feel and live happily.

X

SACRIFICE AT THE ALTAR

IF you have followed me with interest, I think it must have dawned on you, and you must have realized, that to enter this abode of Happiness you must be free from all those things that fetter, that keep you down to the earth—to the sorrows, to the pleasures, and to the various turmoils; and that to escape from them and to be liberated means enlightenment, the attainment of Nirvana, the obeying of that one Law and the entering into that one and absolute Kingdom of Happiness. It means also that you must be free of karma; it means that in the past, over which now you have no control, you may have committed errors and so-called sins, made bad judgments, which have brought in their wake the fetters and sorrows which karma always brings. But over the present and the future you have power; you can control the future by the present, and thus eliminate the illusion of time and space. You, who are trying to understand, who are trying to reach this abode, who are trying to be part of this realm where there is Eternal Happiness, must realize that neither in the present nor in the future should you accumulate more karma, should you create new barriers between yourself and your goal. That means that you must watch, that you must be full of self-recollection, full of solemn and joyful examination of yourself, so that whatever your feelings, whatever your thoughts, whatever your deeds, they may in no way bar your entrance to that Kingdom. The gates of that Kingdom are not shut—for there are no real gates to that Kingdom, no barriers; it is you who create the barriers, the gates, and the gate-keeper. You can only control karma by careful thought, by introspection, by examination of all the little things of life, of all your thoughts and your happiness and the pleasures of your daily life.

Introspection does not mean morbidity or self-centeredness or being engrossed in yourself and excluding every one else; this faculty should help you to cultivate, and encourage you to grow, your mental, emotional, and physical bodies according to the one supreme desire. Like a vine, whose instinct is to grow in all directions instead of along one particular path, you will tend more and more to wander, unless, like a wise gardener, you control your mind and your heart as he would control the vine.

Introspection, as I said, must not tend towards morbidity or depression; this faculty should be used with absolute impersonal feeling, like a student who goes through his daily routine to achieve his end. Without introspection, without this solemn questioning and cross-examination, you do not build character; and without character, without qualities well-developed to their fullest extent, logically and systematically, you will be like dead wood, without life, without the inherent qualities that are necessary for those who wish to follow, to create, to live nobly.

Each one of you must be capable of offering something at the altar, each one of you must bring flowers in your basket when you come to the temple—flowers fully blossomed, giving out their delicious fragrance, beauteous and dignified. When you arrive with such flowers at the altar, then you will be acceptable men; if you arrive with a basket but with no flowers, and are willing merely to adore in a sentimental fashion, without divine capacities well-developed, you will be useless. You must have something to give. You cannot merely say: "I have given myself." Every one of us can say that, because we possess very little to give. It is like a man who has nothing that says: "I give up the world." But if a man of experience, if a man who has understood and conquered the world, if such a man gives up his riches, his glories, then his renunciation has value; because he has experience, has suffered, and his giving up becomes an example to all. When the man who has no roses in his garden says, "I give up all that I possess," it has but little value; because his devotion and his intelligence are backward; and when such a person offers to give up, there is no beauty in his gesture. Whereas if a man of intelligence, of devotion, energy, and power, gives up everything and follows his ideal, that man will be acceptable.

Though you may not have great capacities, may not have great intelligence or be full of devotion, or have immense energy, you can at least offer a formed character, a definite deed, a flower which you have cultivated in your own garden, which you have kept alive through troublous times. When you come to the altar with such a gift, however small it is, it is of value, because it means that you have learned to give those things that are acceptable, that are worthy, that are dignified. And as I said before, a time must come, a time will come, when that Voice, that Tyrant, will tell you to give up everything and follow; and for that time you must be prepared. You must have your garden well weeded and cultivated and its flowers ready to be plucked. Then you can give of your devotion, of your intelligence, with greater certainty, with greater knowledge that it will be used, because you have trained it, because you have cultivated it, because you know what are its capacities; and you yourself are then the master of these things. And when you make a sacrifice—if it can be called a sacrifice, because you are following your own delight, your own happiness, and in that there is no sacrifice—when you come with these flowers to the temple, then the High Priest of that temple, who is your own inner Voice, your own Ruler, your own Lawgiver, will take these and will use them, nourish them, and make them more beautiful, and breathe on them and give them Divinity.

[89]

While you are still wandering and groping, it is essential that you should be all the time forming this character, that you should be ripening this fruit, so that when the time comes it may be plucked, it may give nourishment and delight to others. For this reason it is that self-recollectedness, that constant watchfulness, constant wakefulness, is so necessary. We must not go to sleep, but we can dream; we must keep awake, but we can have our own quiet visions. The more you are watching, the more you are alert, the better you can fight the little things that create karma, that bind you to this wheel of birth and death, to this turmoil, to this everlasting something that gives sorrow. By throwing off all these things you can live in that Kingdom; and you can only do it if you have the mind well-trained and cultivated, the emotions well-nourished and refined, and a body that is well-subjugated.

This self-recollection, this introspection, this examination of all things small or big, must be done every day; and so you must meditate, you must think, you must ponder, in order that every day those little barriers, little weaknesses, may disappear; and thus through meditation you can create. It is the same with emotion; you must purify it, make it impersonal, make it strong, and remove from it any tinge of pettiness, of selfishness, of jealousy, of little angers, and all little disturbances that grow into great barriers. Your mind and your emotions must function with perfect ease. And when you have such a mind and such emotions, it is very easy to control your body; it is very easy to detach yourself from the bodily desires, wants, sufferings, and to treat it as you would treat a beautiful garment. If you will pardon my talking about a personal affair—I remember when I was at Ooty, in the Nilgiris in India, I was experimenting with myself, not very successfully at first, trying to discover how I could detach myself and see the body as it is. I had been experimenting with it for two or three days, it may have been a week; and I found that for a certain length of time I could quite easily be away from the body and look at it. I was standing beside my bed, and there was the body on the bed—a most extraordinary feeling. And from that day there has been a distinct sense of detachment, of division between the ruler and the ruled,

[91]

so that the body, though it has its cravings, its desires to wander forth and to live and enjoy separately for itself, does not in any way interfere with the true self. And that is why you must train all your bodies—mental, emotional, and physical—to have an independent existence of their own, and yet to be coöperative. So that the mind can say to the emotions: You shall feel such and such a thing, and you shall go so far and no further. And the same demands the emotions can make of the body. So you are three different beings; and you have much more fun, there is a much more adventurous spirit in this knowledge. Instead of being one person, you are three separate beings; so that you have the point of view of three, the karma of three, and interests of three, the delights of three. You thus learn to become part of the world, part of the whole system, instead of being one particular individual; so that you lose yourself, your three selves, in the innumerable millions of selves. They are all struggling along the same lines, though expressing themselves in different ways. And if you can experience this delight, if you can train all these three beings, you will be free from many of the fetters of your karma; you will find that you are liberated, that you can wander away from all things, that you can enter and abide forever in that Kingdom. It gives you a different understanding, different delights, a different breath of life. You want to taste the sorrows of experience, you want to imbibe, you want to learn, you want to observe, you want to do all things and yet be free from the fetters which they bring in their wake. You are an outside observer, using discrimination, weighing, balancing, and judging; and if you are able to do that all day long and every second, not with too much seriousness, not with a lack of humor, you will find that the gates of this abode are open and that you can wander in and out, that you can sit down and worship where and when you like. And that is the only pleasure in life, the only delight that an intelligent man can possibly have; for after all, an intelligent man can never be satisfied for very long with the world—he must have something beyond, he must have dreams, he must have visions, he must have great longings. And though very few of us are really intelligent, though very few of us have this sense of adventure, of longing to discover something new, we can always create it; we can always break down the barriers, and open the shutters which keep away the light, which hide away the Truth. And then we can take a delight, a real pleasure, in dreaming, in having great visions; because those dreams and those visions are the Truth, they are the realities, they are the nourishment, and by that alone we can live, by that alone we can survive. We must have dreams, we must have visions. However practical, however direct we may be, we must have this mysticism, this life hidden away from all. We must have our own canvas on which we are painting a picture that we are improving and altering through Eternity, which always gives us the satisfaction of creating, of renewing, of doing what we really desire to do; and which guards us against that terrible thing, self-satisfaction, that sense of always remaining in the same circle, in the same fold. That is the only Truth that any one of us need possess. Once we have entered, once we have seen, once we have dreamed, we can always go back and live in our Kingdom.

XI

THE ENCHANTED GARDEN

I WISH I could make you enter the Kingdom of Happiness, live in that reality, breathe that air of immense purity, and make you enjoy yourself, delight yourself, in that Kingdom. I wish I could make you enter into my heart and my mind, and make you see things as they are, make you feel the world as it is and live with me in all those things which are really lasting and permanent. I do not want you, or ask you, or urge you, or in any way **force** you to wander into unknown fields, to delight in things which are not known, which are not experienced, which are not remembered. It is because you yourself know of this Eternal Abode, of this Truth, of these realities—it is because you have yourself visited this Kingdom, lived in it, revelled in it, delighted in it—that I want you to remain in that Kingdom, that world which is real; to wander in it, and then come back into this world which is unreal, which is transient, to live here constantly in the Real. Most of us go out into the true Kingdom, the Reality, as though it were something strange, as though we were entering into something unknown; whereas *this* world of sense is the unknown, the passing, the trivial, the thing that does not matter in the least.

If once you have entered, if once you have breathed the freshness, the quietness, the tranquillity of this Kingdom, then those things which are real, those things which are the breath of life, those things that matter, can never be forgotten. You can never doubt, you can never suffer again. It is only then you can know that you are not blindly following the footsteps of another; it is only then that you are following the Absolute, the Eternal. It is only then that you are one with Him who has His being in all things. It is only then that you can persuade, can have the tongue of the learned, the heart of the wise and the compassionate. It is only then that you can make people really know what it means to escape from sorrow, from all those trivial things by which they are harrowed and ground down in their daily lives. That is why you must find yourself, that is why you must listen to that Voice, why you must suffer and learn by every little thing in daily life. For when once you have found yourself, you have found Him; and He becomes part of you, becomes one with you, He is where you are and not a separate entity, a separate Being, living in solitary radiance. Where you are, there He is, and where I am, there He is, and when any one has lived and delighted in that Kingdom, He is with him. Because you have found yourself, you have found the true Self; and once you have found Him, you can always return to the Source. You have then the key to all knowledge, you have always the power to be part of the Eternal compassion, the Eternal source of all things. I wish I had the power to make you look at things, feel things, for yourself.

Yesterday I was sitting on the Avenue in front of this Castle.* You know how the trees here grow, some short, some tall, and how together they form a cave round about the trunks; and there I saw my Glory, my Happiness, everything that to me is real, the source, the life, of all trees, of all living things. When once you can see Him, live in Him, and have your being in Him, you are then eternally in

* Castle of Eerde, Ommen, Holland.

[97]

that garden, and not an outsider looking at a few tree trunks, a few roses, a few flowers.

There are two types of people: those who are in this garden where there is lusciousness, freshness, beauty, the tranquillity, and the gentle murmur of a thousand voices; where the whole air is alive with the sense of Eternal Beauty, where there is the sense of power, the sense of peace and of astonishing strength and reality. The other type are those who are outside this garden merely looking at the tree tops, the few stray flowers, where there are hardly any shadows, where there is thin foliage and a few dead branches of last season. Once you have entered this garden, you can give others the key and persuade them to enter for themselves. You can make them realize that this garden, this Kingdom, has no barriers, though it may have a superficial wall made by human thoughts and human feelings. Once you are inside it, you are no longer looking at the inside world from the outside, but are looking at the outside world from the Truth, from the source of all things, from the true self. Once you have this key, you can always go outside, look at the thin foliage, see the dead branches, the remains of last season's withered flowers; you can always then go outside and have experience, for you have entered that garden and have found there the true knowledge, the true Happiness.

That is why, had I the power, I would drag you all in by force or by any other means, because when once you have looked into the garden and caught but a fleeting vision, you will never be satisfied by the outside effect of things; you will always want to go back, always want to have that vision enlarged, glorified, and extended; you will have a thousand terrors haunting you if you are outside. The moment you enter this abode of the Eternal, those terrors, those things that do not matter, those doubts, those worries, those passing sufferings, will all vanish away; because then you will be living in the hidden world where only a few, only the real sufferers, the real seekers after knowledge, the real believers, the real searchers live. Into that world you must go, because that is the only world that is lasting, because it is the only world where you can find Truth. In other worlds you are bound to create sorrows, superstitions, dogmas, and all the unrealities that each one of us creates. In that world you cease to exist as an individual. You are part of everything, part of the smallest leaf and of the tallest and greatest tree; because you are part of Him, and it is His garden, it is His abode, it is His Kingdom. It is where we must all live, where I live. We must all be thrilled by the same Voice. You can see how much more inspiring, desirable, and adventurous, that world is in comparison with this world. But to attain it, you must train yourself, you must have that Voice so attuned, so purified, so incessant, that it urges you on and on till you enter this Kingdom, this garden, the beauty spot of the world—of all the worlds.

Because it is my abode, because it is my source, I would I could make you live with me, I would I could share with each one of you what I have found. When once you have tasted it for yourself, as I have tasted it for myself, you can never completely lose it but will always find it again. If you have not searched for it, struggled to attain it, you cannot know what it means, cannot know the power of it, the stimulating ambitions, the ecstasy, the intoxication. It is not mere sentiment, mere emotion, but it is the very Truth, it is the essence of all things; and that is why it is so vital, so real—that is why, if you would do great things, if you would create greatly and live nobly, you must enter that Kingdom, live in that garden, enjoy the shades of that garden and the scent of many flowers and the murmurings of many bees. To live in that garden means that you live greatly, you live nobly, to the height of your perfection; and whatever is done greatly and lastingly must be done from that abode, must start from that source, must have its origin in that Kingdom. All trials, attempts, and deeds, fail when they are not lasting, when they are transient and changeable. Whereas if everything that you do bears the seal of this Kingdom, it will be acceptable to all men, to all gods, to all the kingdoms of Nature; because this Kingdom is the realm of gods, the realm of ideals, the source of all feelings, of all actions.

You must know for yourself why you seek this garden, this abode; and once you know that, you need not struggle to cling to it—it will never leave you. You need not fear that it will escape you, that it will vanish away through your foolish actions, small desires, and little worries. Like a beautiful image or a lovely vision, it always comes back in moments of tranquillity, or of great uncertainty. You will always have this as your background; you can always retire to that garden, you can always escape from this unreal world.

You must find yourself, you must make this Voice thunder out. You must have a thousand terrors, must have innumerable questionings, until you find that Voice. Till then there must be no peace, no tranquillity, no contentment, no happiness. All other things are unreal. This is the greatest of ideals, the essence of intelligence.

Have you ever seen how the pools and still waters, under perfectly clear skies, reflect every little shadow, every bird that passes by, and every cloud that is driven by the gentle breeze? Suddenly a little insect comes by and disturbs the stillness of the water, and that vision is gone. That little insect on the surface of the water disturbs the whole beauty of the world; and then it disappears and once more there is the tranquillity, the calm, the perfect purity of reflection. You must re-remove that little insect; it must be ruthlessly slain; it is the separate self.

As long as you can reflect with the certainty, with the knowledge, that your reflection is as perfect as the Kingdom itself—as long as you can be that reflection itself—no little insect, no passing wind, can ruffle the still waters of your life; you can only reflect the purity of that Kingdom when you have found your true Self, when you live eternally in your Kingdom and have Him as your eternal Companion. Then you have in you that absolute peace, the peace that gives enormous strength and power, because you have found yourself, because you have lived with those things that are permanent, that are eternal, that are worth possessing. I wish I could stir you to action so that you must create, you must dream, you must perceive, you must live. But you must bestir yourself; you must apply the whip yourself; and you can only feel the sting of that whip, when you hear that Voice. That Voice is ever calling, ever insistent; and the greater the thundering of the Voice, the greater will be the nobility of your actions, the greater will be your strength and the greater your desire to enter into that garden, that Kingdom of Happiness.

XII

THE ETERNAL COMPANION

As thunder is born of power, threat, and mystery, so is the Voice of Truth in a strong man. As the voice of thunder is thrown from mountain to mountain and as each mountain catches it and returns it to the other, so is the Voice of Him—our Ruler, our Lawgiver, our Guide and Friend—in the man who is following the absolute Truth, the Truth of his own creation. Like the mountain, so full of unified strength, so full of power, so full of dignity, of that sense of majesty, so is the man who has found himself, who has created his own ideal, who is striding towards his own goal. Such a man is worthy, such a man is acceptable, such a man must be the leader of men, must create, must renew and give strength to those who are weak, to those that are in the valley, to those that are in the plains, where the thunder is not so powerful as in those mountains, where the strong man only can enjoy and really appreciate the sense of tremendous awe. But a weak man, a man of the plains, to him the sense of beauty, the voice of thunder, will not convey the same meaning. The strong man must be the leader, must be the joyous one, because to him that Voice, that beauty, that power, and that strength, mean the end of the search and the beginning of a new life. Such a strong man must be as joyous as those treetops, those delicate branches, those few leaves that are the playthings of the passing winds, those leaves that are the delight of the sun, and those leaves that dance in ecstasy in that brilliancy because they are nearer heaven. There is in them no struggle, no fatigue; though full of vital power, yet they are yielding, and know not what it means to resist. They are unconscious of the roots that give them strength, that keep them alive, that grow deep down into the earth that struggle and grow continuously, and that have great agonies because they have to nourish such great heights. Such strength, such power to struggle, such power to give energy for creation is the Kingdom of Happiness. If a man would find such strength and at the same time such joyousness, such struggle and at the same time such ecstasy in life, such growth and at the same time the perfect form—such a man will find that he has within him an eternal Companion, such a man will find that, wherever he is, wherever he lives, wherever he breathes, he is not alone, that loneliness does not know him, nor does any extreme; but that he is walking joyously in that middle path that leads to the Kingdom of Heaven. Then he will find, as so many Indians who love Shri Krishna have found: that because they wanted Him to be their companion, because they had in their hearts an eternal longing to be with Him, He appeared to each one of them, He was their companion, their delight, their oblivion, and He appeared different according to the evolution of each, according to the evolution of the mind and of the heart of each. He was what they made Him, He was what they wanted Him to be—either the God or a simple friend, either the great Dancer or a lazy companion, either the great creator or a feeble destroyer. His outward form depended on the minds of those who longed, and on the hearts of those who had suffered and found a new breath in life.

Such must be the case with each one of us

[106]

who are seeking Him, the embodiment of the Kingdom of Happiness. He appears to us as we want Him to appear; He is as we are; He is as we make Him to be. That is the reason that, so long as there is this longing, this desire to be with Him, this desire to know Him, to exult in Him, so long as there is this desire, it does not matter what our stage of evolution may be. This is the only vital truth in life. For He is the embodiment of all; and as long as we understand in our heart the essence of this Truth, in its simplicity, we are with Him eternally. But first there must be that desire, that tremendous longing, that intense burning, till we find that garden where we can create our own image of Him who is Eternal.

For some months past I have searched for Him in all things, I have always desired to see things through Him. My eyes must be His eyes and I must see all things, whether they be small or big, whether they be dead or alive, through Him. That desire has been growing in intensity, that desire has become my breath; and like so many ancient Indians, so many mystics the world over, who really longed for Truth, who really searched and suffered and found Him, like them I found

Him. And ever since then I have lived in that garden of many roses, many scents; and being in ecstasy I breathe that scented air, the only air that makes me grow, gives me power, gives me strength and vitality—to my mind, my heart, to my very being. And, possessing such strength, I can only give and not withhold.

A few days ago, I went for a stroll; and while I walked, I walked with Him who is my Eternal Companion. I walked a while and I sat down under a tree, not thinking of any thing but this one thing; and I looked, and there He was in front of me, sitting; and then I saw how Nature worships Him. The trees and the little blades of grass and the wind that blew, all were worshiping Him. And as I looked, and as my soul gathered strength in ecstasy, and as my body thrilled, forever, I was aware, I was like Him; there was no difference, I was part of Him; I could not distinguish a different entity; I could not disassociate myself from the Eternal. And as I breathed the same air as He, I understood and know what it means to live in that Kingdom of Happiness, to live and play under the shadows in that garden; I knew what it means to look at the flowers and at the other travelers on the road. Everything became part of Him because all those who seek, all those who suffer, all those who are happy, are eternally His; and being in Him, I understood. And that is why all of us who have that tremendous sense of longing after Truth, must realize that without Him, the embodiment of Truth, we do not understand, without Him we do not conquer the self; and we must have Him in the center of our being, for then we can go away from the center like the sparks that rush forth from the flame.

While I was in that state—nothing extraordinary, nothing abnormal or supernatural—while I was in that supreme ecstasy, I found that there were no barriers between myself and the Kingdom of Happiness; I had removed all the veils that hide the Holy of Holies; I had entered that garden, and had torn aside the veils that hide and distort and cover up that image, that perfection. And if you would follow, realizing that following does not mean blindness, then let us walk together and be companions together. I will show you that fair Vision of that enchanted garden, that Kingdom of Happiness, that abode where there is Eternity, that temple where there is the Holy of Holies. But you must have the eyes to see, you must have the mind well cultivated, refined and capable of great judgment, your heart must be full of that vast love, that impersonal love, that love which knows no barriers, no distinctions, no prejudices; and you must have the strength to work, to step high or step low, either to climb the tremendous heights or to walk in the hot plains; and you must have a soul prepared for temptation, you must have many terrors; you must have no contentment; and above all you must have that greatness, which comes of vast experience, to appreciate the beauty of life in that garden. And if you will follow me to that garden, if you will search for the Truth in that garden, you will find the simple Truth there, you will find the purest the sweetest, the noblest nectar of the Gods. This is the only Truth, the only altar at which you must worship; and that is the conclusion of the whole matter.

The simplest truth can only be attained through vast experience, can only come through ecstasy of love, through immense devotion; and you will find in it the only refuge where you can shelter from all rains and hot days, from all struggles, sorrows, and pain. And once you have found it, there is no question of doubting or even hesitating, because you are then the Master, you are then the ideal of thousands, the helper of many, and you are then the signpost of those that grope, for those that do not see, that are still struggling in the darkness. And once we can walk together on that path of eternal peace that leads to that Kingdom of Happiness, then there is no question of separation, no question of loneliness, no doubt of attainment—that attainment which is perfection, which is enlightenment; because then you are the embodiment of all those things which each one of you seeks. And when you walk on that road and sport yourselves in that eternal garden, when you can shelter yourself in the shades away from the sun, then we are all friends, then we are all eternal companions, then we are all creating, in the image of Him who is the Holy of Holies. And when once you have drunk this nectar, this elixir of life, it keeps you eternally young; though you may have had vast experiences, though you may have shed many tears, have suffered greatly, there is inside you the bubbling spring-well that keeps you eternally full, eternally young and joyous, like the dancing star in a dark night; because you know all, and the self, which is the destroyer of Truth, the perverter of Truth, is annihilated.

And so you must all, if you would follow me—you must all walk to that gate, that gate that keeps you away from that eternal garden, and there you will find the many keys, and each one of you can take a key and enter. But you must have that immense delight, that immense pleasure, before you can enter that Kingdom of Happiness; and then you will realize that you are the Master, and that the wheel of birth and death has ceased. There you will find the Eternal Refuge, the Eternal Truth; and there you will lose the identity of your separate self; and there you will create new worlds, new kingdoms, new abodes for others.

CPSIA information can be obtained
at www.ICGtesting.com
Printed in the USA
LVHW061456070420
652487LV00016B/1365